# The Eternal Prank

## Myth, Satire and Drama

Erminio G. Neglia

First Edition
Biographical Publishing Company
Prospect, Connecticut

# The Eternal Prank
## Myth, Satire and Drama
### First Edition

Published by:

**Biographical Publishing Company**
35 Clark Hill Road
Prospect, CT 06712-1011
Phone: 203-758-3661   Fax: 253-793-2618
e-mail: biopub@aol.com

All rights reserved. No part of this book may be reproduced or transmitted in any form or by any means, electronic or mechanical, including photocopying, recording, or by any information storage or retrieval system without the written permission of the author, except for the inclusion of brief quotations in a review.

Copyright © 2007 by Erminio G. Neglia
First Printing 2007

**PRINTED IN THE UNITED STATES OF AMERICA**

Publisher's Cataloging-in-Publication Data

Neglia, Erminio G.
The Eternal Prank : Myth, Satire and Drama/ by Erminio G. Neglia.--
1st ed. p. cm.
1. Erminio G. Neglia
Title: stories and plays. II. Title.
ISBN 1-929882-44-0
13 Digit ISBN 9781929882441
Dewy Decimal classifications: 814
Library of Congress Control Number: 2007928185

# Dedication

This book is dedicated to my family and, in particular, to my understanding wife Ligia.

## Table of Contents

Stories.............................................. 5

Here, All Together, Keeping Company.............. 36

The Case of Clara Bellucci........................ 51

My place of birth does not exist; at least according to the maps of Italy I have seen. According to them I was born between a dot and a little circle, the dot indicating a big city and the little circle a town. Why my town with more than 35000 people does not appear on any map is really a mystery. So when they ask me where I was born, I answer that I was born between a dot and a little circle somewhere on the Adriatic coast of Italy.

I can't say, however, that it's a pretty town. They have built so much that now it's a jungle of cement buildings. None of the nice red-tiled roofs of many Italian towns you see in postcards. An impressionistic view from the air would look like a grey and white smear on a canvas.

I was born with a name that does not exist. Let me explain. It does not appear on any calendar. All my friends at school would ask me when was my saint's name celebrated. I was invited to their parties and they expected me to invite them to my party to celebrate my name day. The truth is there is no saint by that name. I had to invent a date on my own calendar. The date was chosen carefully to avoid any conflict with a well known saint's date.

I think I was too hard on my hometown (you are critical of people and places you love most because you want them to be better or at least the way they were. That's why I hate Berlusconi for what he has done to Italy.) So my hometown is not all that bad. There is a tiny patch of green, the Villa as they call it, and a fairly big cathedral with some famous paintings. Above all, my town is not too far from the sea and that's a plus, for in the hot days of summer, in twenty minutes you can go and plunge in the Adriatic Sea. Also, in the jungle of cement, some old houses have been preserved. When I look at them now I remember the way it was. The wagons were pulled by mules going and returning from the fields. Before the invasions of cars, streets at dusk would be flanked by the wagons parked in front of the houses. The mules were pulled down in the stables under the house. One man down at the landing of the steep stairs would pull the animal while another man would control his descent by holding on his tail. The smell of hay and the mules' sweat would permeate the street.

Above the entrance to the underground stables there was a narrow cleft for the swallows' nests. The swallows would come back every spring and they were always welcomed.

If the swallows were welcomed, not so the bats. We would try to hit them with stones. Their zigzag flight made our aim difficult. We would end up with one or two a night. During the day, when not in school, we would hunt lizards with loops at the end of long stems cut from the tall grass on the side of deserted streets. The loop would fasten tight once they were caught in it. We would play with them before we killed them with stones. These were some of our diversions during the war years. We also threw stones at stray cats and dogs.

Our cruelty to animals probably stemmed from our anxiety about the war and the incomprehension of why men were cruel to other men.

My town didn't experience the destruction of other places. The sounds of war came mostly from the city, particularly from its port. I was ten or eleven at that time.

When we heard the sirens we ran out to an empty lot across from our house. Two women, mother and daughter who lived next door, rushed with us to take cover behind a stone wall of the empty lot. When we heard the sirens or the planes fly over, the mother, a very heavy lady in her sixties, would always look for me; she would grab me and would go down pulling me on top of her. When the bombs sounded closer she would squeeze me so tight that I almost suffocated, for my face would usually end up between her huge breasts. I tried everything to keep her away from me. I would wear smelly clothes and filled my pockets with pointed pieces of wood and nails. Nothing worked. Then one evening, before rushing out at the sound of the sirens, I inflated a small balloon and hid it in my pants. It was dark and nobody could see my bulging pants. When I was on the ground with her in a tight embrace I blew the balloon with a nail I carried in my hands. The sound scared her to death. She screamed and covered her head with her hands releasing me from her grip. She never grabbed me again. Her daughter was more gentle; she never squeezed me like her mother.

---

After the war, Italy picked herself up from the ruins. The cars replaced the wagons and the mules and my parents' income grew rapidly. I was in my teens and much interested in soccer and girls. My friends and I also liked to play pranks. Pino was the most creative in finding victims. He had an innate gift to determine which weaknesses to exploit. The first victim was Michele who worked in a mill loading sacks of wheat and flour. Around four, he would go to his small parcel of land just outside the town and worked until dark clearing it with his hoe, burning the weeds. His manicured lot was completely devoid of stones of any kind. He would take pains to pick up every single one. The lot was so smooth and flat that it would have been great as a Bocce court. In the early spring he would use one small part of the land to plant vegetables and grow wheat on the rest. Before the green shoots appeared the four of us, with Pino leading, would go and hide behind one of the walls surrounding the lot. We always made sure Michele was there. Then we would stand up and, in unison ,cast a volley of stones onto the field. Imagine Michele's fury! He ran after us while swearing and shouting threats. We repeated this adventure many times. He never caught us but one day Pino, who had lingered behind to throw more stones, was almost apprehended. He didn't expect Michele to climb over the wall so rapidly. He got away but I think Michele had a chance to see his face.

Pino always looked for simple-minded people like Michele. They would believe anything you said. It took them a long time to understand that you want to make fun of them.

Michele had a nickname: Poh Poh I. We didn't know who invented it. It didn't mean anything, it just sounded funny. Michele got furious any time he heard it and that's why we enjoyed using it.

We would meet him in the villa( the only green space in town with a few trees and wide walkways) and we would engage him in a normal conversation. Of course Pino would not participate for fear of being recognized. Michele was not married and lived with his very old mother. We met him in the villa during the weekends. We asked about his plot of land, his work in the mill, his old mother. We talked to him for about half hour before starting to call him Poh Poh I in a muffled way. At that point we were ready to run if he understood the prank. When everybody began to shout the nickname all hell broke loose and we ran for our life.

One day Michele was sitting outside the barber shop when he saw Pino passing by. I was told that in an instant Michele went to Pino, grabbed him by the throat and lifted him up. It took two men to loosen his grip. Michele had recognized him as one of the band of teenagers who liked to throw stones on his land. He had not forgotten.

Many years later, I went back to my hometown. I was walking around the Villa with my friends when I saw an old man all shriveled up sitting on a bench. Then, as we passed by him, I heard him say: "figli di puttana." I was shocked. I asked my friends who he was and why he swore at us. They replied that he was Poh Poh I and that he never forgot.

---

Another of our victims was Luciano. He was in his thirties and very slim. We knew him well because he liked to organize soccer tournaments. He had the time to dedicate to soccer because he never had a steady job. He had some land with some olive trees and grapevines and he owned his own house where he lived alone.

We liked to visit him often because of his strange way of looking at life and, as Michele, he was a simple-minded fellow. He was the butt of many jokes.

He was proud of some grape clusters he brought from his land. He would hang them high up from the ceiling and they were really big. He liked to show us one in particular. He said it weighted six kilos.

One of his enjoyable moments was to sit with a sandwich and a bottle of wine in front of him and look at his bunches of grapes, in particular at the big one.

We decided to steal it. We knew where he hid the key. Next day we all went to the Coffee Shop where we used to meet him. He came in, ordered coffee and stood at the counter without saying a word. After a few minutes of silence, he said that whoever did it was a scoundrel and deserved to be punished. We showed surprise and asked information. We told him how sorry we were, for the big bunch meant a lot to him.

We promised to find out who did it. He said that he sat as usual with his sandwich and the wine. When he looked up at the bunches everything seemed normal. It was only when he was about to leave to go buy some cigarettes that he realized that the heaviest bunch was missing. He couldn't believe it. He went back and sat in the same position before looking up again. No, it was not an hallucination. It was gone. It took all our will power to keep from burst laughing.

We were ready for something more daring. In town there was a lot of talk about a gang who would rob people after making them fall off their bikes. Their fall would be caused by the impact with a thick cable pulled tight from both sides of a road by members of the gang. This would take place at night and the robbers would conceal their identity by wearing masks. They were called "the gang of the cable."

We knew that Luciano sometimes would come back from the fields late at night. We set the trap some distance from town in a deserted part of the road and waited. As he got close we stretched the cable across the street a meter above the ground. We heard him whistling a tune, probably to keep his spirit up. The bike hit the cable throwing Luciano off the saddle. With our heads covered in balaclavas we approached him who was still on the floor. He begged to spare his life. He said he had a wife and five children. He was a poor man but he would give us his bike and all the money he had on him. He took out a few coins. We were about to burst laughing so we let him go after he promised not to say anything in town. He thanked us and took off at full speed.

Next morning, in the Coffee Shop, he told everybody the story of his encounter with the bandits. The ambush did not work. He pedalled so hard that he was able to break through dragging cable and bandits for ten meters. He called them "losers."

We weren't finished with him. The next prank needed the cooperation of many people including the mailman, the police and a translator. Luciano wanted to emigrate to the States. His sister who lived there had a plan: he would go there as a tourist, marry an American citizen and become a resident.

One of our friend who was studying English wrote a letter in English addressed to Luciano. We enclosed a picture of a beautiful actress and we glued a used American stamp on the envelope. The day after the delivery we congregate in the Coffee Shop waiting for him. He walked in with a radiant smile weaving the letter in the air. He asked our friend the translator to translate the letter. It said that she was anxious to meet him in the States. She had heard many good things about him from his sister and she thought he was her type, etc.,etc. She also signed the picture. Luciano was in heaven. He order drinks for everyone. I saw an old man drinking three shots of brandy. He went around showing the picture to each one. He then kissed it and put it back into the envelope. We all congratulate him and one by one left the shop to meet outside and laugh our hearts out.

---

Another simple-minded person we liked to pick on was Ciccillo, although he showed more shrewdness than Luciano and Michele.

He lived with Filomena, his wife, on a small farm. He came to town once in a while, when he could get away from Filomena.

I and two friends were at the usual Coffee Shop when he came in. He took off his hat and put it on the counter and asked for a glass of water. We told Berto, the bartender, to serve him a glass of wine instead.

"OK, but my wife doesn't like me drinking during the day," he paused a second. "Oh, well, she is not here," he raised the glass. " To hell with the women!" And gulped it down.

"We drink with you, Ciccillo. Cheers and to hell with the women!" One of us said and we raised our glasses. Three women sitting at a table gave us a dirty look but they knew what we were up to and kept quiet.

"We heard that to celebrate your birthday they took you to the theatre in the city to see Otello. Was it the first time you went the Opera?"

"Yes, the first time. The theatre was beautiful and everybody was elegant."

"Were you also elegant?"

"Yes, I wore my best suit. The last time I wore it was at the funeral of Contacessi. My shoes were a little tight but I couldn't wear my working boots."

"Tell us how it went."

"Not so well."

"What do you mean? It didn't go well for Desdemona and Otello, we know."

"Also for what happened after the Opera."

"Tell us everything from the beginning, please." We signalled to Berto to leave the bottle of wine in front of him so he could help himself.

He said he didn't understand what they were saying, specially because he was very high up, but he grasped the important events of the story. He finished the third glass of wine.

"It's the story of the handkerchief."

We looked at each other and at the women in bewilderment.

He went on to explain the story. Otello gave Desdemona, his wife, an embroidered handkerchief as a present. Otello was a dark-skinned man and Ciccillo believed that mixed marriages don't work.

By now Ciccillo was drunk. His voice, his red face and his gestures revealed his state of drunkenness. Surreptitiously we waved at Berto for another bottle of wine.

He continued. At a party in the Captain's house Desdemona dropped her handkerchief. At home one night Otello asked her for the handkerchief to dry his forehead. Of course, she didn't have it. The wife ran to the bathroom a brought him a towel. Otello asked her what had happened to the handkerchief. She blushed embarrassed. Otello became suspicious.

"What a wicked woman! You have to be vigilant. You can't trust women," one of us said. The women at the table showed their annoyance with us with silent hostile gestures.

After another drink and a short pause he went on saying that we needed to understand the importance of the handkerchief at the time of Otello. Nobody let the house without it. It would have felt like going around naked. Also at that time it was customary between lovers to exchange handkerchiefs. He learned from Don Vincenzo, with whom he talked about the Opera; he explained to him that the exchange was a way of spreading germs. It got so bad in our town that it was forbidden for fear of epidemics. Today we use pieces of paper but he never liked them. He still used a cotton handkerchief. He took a huge red one out from the back pocket. Even Filomena, his wife, had one; it was green, he said.

Finally he left the history of the handkerchief to resume the story of Otello. He had become so suspicious of his wife that every time he met an officer he would ask him to show him his handkerchief. He saw the embroidered handkerchief, similar to the one he had given to Desdemona, in the hands of the Captain. He ran to the house mad, grabbed Dedemona by the throat and choked her to death.

"He did the right thing," one of us said. "Cuckholds have to avenge the betrayals. Hurrah for the cuckholds!" We raised our glasses.

"Wait! Wait! It's not finished. Men and women entered the bedroom and saw Desdemona lying dead on the bed. They all started to cry. "It was a mistake! It was a mistake!" They shouted. They told Otello that there were many embroidered handkerchiefs around because a few months before a shipment of them arrived by boat.

"Per la miseria! Desdemona was innocent!" We also cried out.

Ciccillo continued his story. Otello, believing that he had made a big mistake, standing by Desdemona, took out his dagger and plunged it in his stomach, paf!

"Yes, everybody believed that Desdemona was innocent but I didn't." Ciccillo said. We looked at each other in disbelief. The women stirred in their seats.

"But how could the handkerchief in the hands of the Captain be Desdemona's for sure, if there were so many around?"

He explained his point of view: "The Captain blushed when he told the people in the bedroom that he was innocent."

"But how could you see him blush from way up there in the gallery." We asked.

"I borrowed the binoculars from Beppe who was sitting next to me. There was no doubt. She was guilty . . . And that's how it all ended. Two people dead and the Captain, guilty like

Desdemona, alive and well."

He drank some more. During a minute of silence that followed we seriously assessed in our minds the ending of the Opera according to Ciccillo. Then we asked him to tell us what happened to him after the Opera. After the end of Otello everyone was crying including Beppe, his wife and Filomena sitting to his left. All of a sudden, Filomena took out her green handkerchief and pass it to Beppe to his right who was also crying. Ciccillo jumped up and grabbed Beppe by the throat. We asked why. He replied that the damned handkerchief made him feel like Otello, the cuckhold who, instead of killing only his wife, should have killed the Captain also. It took many people to separate them.

We thanked him for the interesting recount of Otello and wished him Happy Birthday. We went to sit at the table with the women. We were drinking wine when Filomena came in. She was a fat and strong woman of around sixty.

"Ciccillo . . . here you are. I knew I would find you here. You've been drinking, right?"

Ciccillo turned around facing her with a ferocious look on his face. "Desdemona, get out! I'll take care of you at home."

Filomena unafraid went to him, took him by the hand and started to walk slowly toward the door. Ciccillo, staggering, didn't oppose any resistance. Berto, the bartender, told Filomena that Ciccillo owed for two bottles of wine. Filomena scornfully answered telling Berto to put the bill on the Mayor's account. Ciccillo stopped to say to us that we had to pay because he had been our guest.

"They made fun of you, didn't they?" She asked, looking at us.

"Yes, but this time I enjoyed myself more than they. I had fun inventing a story. Remember, Filomena, the Opera we were going to see? We didn't go but Don Vincenzo told me the story and I recreated it my own way. . . . I had free drinks thanks to them."

"Yes, you got plastered for free but who is going to milk the cow and clean the stable? There is so much to do and you, instead, come here to tell stories."

"But I only came in to get a glass of water."

The two, hand in hand, walked out leaving us with a feeling of having been taken for a ride. The teasing had backfired

---

I went to the United States in 1956 to study. I didn't get along with my uncle who sponsored me and I found it difficult to pay for the university tuition. So I joined the American Army. We were sent to Fort Belvuoir in Virginia for the training. I studied Water Purification. What a change: from literature at the university to purifying water! I couldn't enter the Officers School because, at that time, my English was not that good. After the course in Water Purification, I was sent to another camp for the drudging drills in warlike games before been shipped out to Korea.

One of the drills was in the forest. We were taken individually into an inextricable part of the forest and left alone with a flashlight and a compass. We were supposed to find our way back to camp. I had heard of this drill from other GIs who had gone through it and I prepared myself. As I walked with the Sargent to the place where he would leave me, along the way I would drop pieces of white cloth on the floor or hang them on bushed and branches. I would also mark tree trunks with a luminous type of markers used by the Army for many purposes. It wasn't difficult for me to find my way back. The

Sargent couldn't believe it.

The other drills were strenuous. I hated especially the long marches under the sun with a heavy load on my back. Then we would camp and sleep in small individual tents. Once, the rain was coming down in torrents and we were all wet. We pitched the tents in the rain and the muck. We had to take turns to keep guard. The Sargent, who went back in a jeep as soon as it started to rain, gave each of us a list with the names of all the ten soldiers in the camp. Each would be on guard duty one hour and when his shift was over he would call the name of the GI next on the list. I was fifth on the list. The rain kept on coming and every hour a new name was called aloud. We were very tired and wet. I heard my name called. The soldier who was calling did not know where my tent was. He kept on calling. The problem was that the name he was calling did not sound like mine. He tried a couple of phonetic sounds that didn't come close to my name. He kept on mispronouncing it for about ten minutes. I decided not to relieve him. My alibi to the Sargent, if he ever would have found out, would have been that I didn't hear my name called. This worked so well that I did it again later on another long march.

I was in Korea about a year. We were stationed near the city of Taegu. The war had ended a few years before. The economical and social damage to the Koreans was evident everywhere. Prostitution and black market were rampant.

I was station in a Military Compound near Taegu. I and another Water Specialist were assigned to a Water Point between the town and the Compound. We had our own barrack and a few meters away there was a shed with the equipment and the machine to purify the water that came from Taegu. A barbed wire fence surrounded the place. On top of the shed there was a huge water tank from which the water flew to the Compound. The problem was that the equipment broke down frequently and nobody knew how to fix it. Our solution was to climb the ladder to the top of the tank and by hand throw in a couple of buckets of chlorine every couple of days. As far as I know, nobody got sick, only a few complaints about the smell of chlorine.

After the military service, I went back to the university. I got my B.A. in Chicago, married a Colombian and after five years of graduate studies I received my Ph.D. in Latin American Literature. I was able to pay the cost of the university and to support my family by teaching as Teaching Assistant and by grants. The GI Bill, designed to help veterans continue their education, also helped.

I got my first job as a professor in Canada. After thirty years of teaching I retired as Professor Emeritus.

---

Although mostly involved in research and teaching, I did find some time for creative writing in fiction and theatre. Since I did it for fun, I didn't have a method, as some writers have. When I knew I could get up late in the morning, I would go to bed with a story on my mind. I would stay awake until I had some idea of the form and content of the story; then I would fall asleep and let my subconscious take over. Usually the subconscious makes a mess of things but in my case it helped, at least in half of my guided dreams. When I knew I had a story, I would refine it and then test it; and that's when my friends come in.

Mario and I had spent a glorious day on Lake Tamani. We celebrated our release from the winter prison of cold and snow with much rejoicing over our good catch. In the evening, on our way home, after arguing about who would clean the fish, we decided to have my wife cook it. She left after supper to go to her sister's house; we sat by the fireplace.

"Come on. I am too tired to hear another of your stories."

I brought him a cognac and he agreed to listen to my story but only if it were short.

"Well, as you know, Mario, us small town boys . . . "

"How many times do I have to tell you . . . I am a city boy. You know . . . paved street, stoplights, pigeons . . . "

"Ya, ya. Whatever. As I was saying, being raised in a small town like mine, I never got a chance to see an airplane up close."

"You 've got to be kidding . . . you never saw an airplane?"

"Well ya, I saw them flying by . . . but to me they were just huge noisy things, I was terrified of them."

"All right, all right . . . you were scared of planes . . . get on with the story."

"OK . . . I told you once how superstitious my mother was. Well, it wasn't just my mother. The whole town was like that."

"Ignorance breeds superstition."

"But ,Mario, I wasn't ignorant. I went to school."

Mario was getting impatient. He wanted to leave. I tried to calm him down by telling him that stories seem unclear in the beginning . . . I offered him another cognac. "My town was full of nuns, monks and priests. I didn't mind the priest or the monks . . . but the nuns! I considered them bad luck. Even today, when I see a nun I scratch myself."

"What do you mean? Just seeing them makes you itchy?"

"No. It's superstition. You see, you have to do something to offset the bad luck, so I scratch my private parts."

"What! You mean you pull down your zipper . . . ?"

"No, silly. That's not necessary. You just stroke them a couple of times over your pants."

Tony burst laughing. He made himself more comfortable in the sofa. He seemed more at ease, more interested.

"A year after my arrival to the U.S.A. I was invited by my uncle to visit him in Seattle. He sent me the money for the plane ticket. You can imagine how I felt. I was scared of planes. It was the first time in my life that I had to take a plane. But the worst thing happened later. At the airport I saw a an old nun right behind me in the line to board the plane."

"So you went for the genitals." He burst laughing again.

"I got on the plane and found my seat. I was fastening my seat belt when I saw her again coming through the isle. I breathed a sigh of relief when she moved ahead past my seat. Then, all of a sudden, she reappeared. Her seat was next to mine. I never felt so miserable in all my life." I threw more wood on the fire. I drank some beer and looked at Mario. He told me to hurry up and finish the story. I told him that I was terrified. The two things I feared most had joined to take hold of my life.

"You can imagine how I felt when that monstrous machine lifted into the air! Anyway, after about an hour, I started to relax. I opened my eyes . . . I should have kept them shut! She smiled at me and asked if it was my fist flight, for I looked too tense. I told her that it was my first and my last. She became serious making me realize that there could have been another meaning to my words. I closed my eyes again. I felt very sleepy . . . Things became blurred, distant, except for those fears inside of me . . .

Then all of a sudden, the plane started to shake. The Captain's voice came over the intercom. One of the engines had caught fire and we were losing altitude fast. A stewardess, in a trembling voice, gave us instructions for a forced landing. A few terrible moments went by. Then the old nun threw herself into my arms, clinging to me desperately. She asked me to hold her tight because she was scared. Then . . . " I paused and looked at Mario.

"You CRASHED!" He said loudly.

For a moment I pondered the solution to my story that Mario had come up with. I didn't like it.

"No, stupid! I wouldn't be here if we had crashed."

"So, what happened?"

"Nothing. I woke up. The plane was about to land. It had been only a bad dream, a nightmare."

Mario jumped up furious and called me all kinds of names. "From now on keep your dreams to yourself. I will never, never listen to your stories again." He left slamming the door behind.

I went to the icebox, took another beer and walked to my desk. Before beginning the task of re-writing the story I considered Mario's reactions. In general, I was pleased. With the exception of some momentary dips, all in all Mario's interest in the story had remained high. Of course, I wondered whether it had been a good idea telling him that I had dreamed it all up. Poor Mario! He was really upset. But then, I could recall reading many stories with the same disturbing ending.

Sitting in front of the computer, I was assailed with the eternal question of how much dialogue I should use in a story like this. I decided to leave that question unanswered until morning; I left the computer and went to bed . . .

I dreamed I had been born in a small town, was afraid of planes and nuns and had told a story to a friend . . .

---

Frank is different. He is more patient than Mario. As a matter of fact, he likes to hear my stories, the craziest the better.

I always dreamed about doing something supernatural. We all dream about flying or about being the best in athletics, the fastest, the strongest . . . Some like me daydream about some magic powers like being able of fixing a stalled car on the side of the road by just willing it in passing by or attracting the interest of a beautiful woman on the beach, and that would really be magic at my age. Lately my imagined magic power was extended to the dogs.

Frank and I were sitting on the patio in my backyard drinking beer. He agreed to listen to my latest story. I warned him that it was a little strange.

"The first time it happened was last fall. I was walking down towards the river when, from nowhere, appeared a huge dog. I froze. He growled and showed his teeth. I didn't know what to do. Running would have been unwise, as it would have been an invitation for him to attack me. I decided to stand firm and look him straight in the eyes. Then surprisingly, out of my mouth came the word "sit." And you know what? He sat; right in front of me and all his aggressiveness had vanished. His owner appeared and excused himself. He said the dog got away suddenly and he ran as fast as he could. I didn't believe him. I told him that the dog should be on the leash at all times.

I continued my walk along the Credit River . . . by the way,

Frank, do you know why it's called "Credit."

"The Indians used to buy on credit from the white men; just go on; forget the river. I think this may be the most interesting of all your boring stories."

"Yes, Frank ,I think you will like it. As I was saying, as I was walking along the Credit River, I thought about the incident of the dog. Why did he obey my command to sit? He didn't know me. Was he used to that command by the owner? Anyway, after a while, I forgot the whole thing until a month later. A lady came to my house. I let her in. She was from the Animal Service and she wore a uniform. She said I hadn't paid for the dog's license. I said I had. While we were arguing, my dog appeared and I, concerned about the lady, said: "sit!" Of course the dog sat as he had been trained to do. But what was strange was that the woman sat down on the floor also. I helped her up. She said she just felt sitting down. She was all confused and forgot about our argument.

You see, Frank, that's when I realized that there was something magical about the word "sit" uttered by me. What was even stranger was that it affected both animals and people.

As you can imagine, the news of my strange power spread throughout our neighborhood and beyond."

"How come I didn't hear anything?"

"Be quiet and listen. It was weird seeing dogs sitting down at the end of my driveway when going by with their owners who, fortunately, did not feel the same urge to sit as their pets. Probably they also would have sat if I had given the command. The dogs felt my magic power even at a distance.

One day the lady of the big house at the corner invited me in to see me work the prodigy on her German Shepherd. As soon as I walked in I heard the dog growling and coming towards me. She held him back by the collar. As he got closer, I said, "sit!" And he sat but so did the lady. I looked at her bare legs and she covered them up in a hurry. I helped her up. She was amazed at what she saw. She gave me a drink and asked if she could invite friends with their dogs so that I could show them my prodigious act. I declined. Anyway I started to receive many requests. One was from a circus and another from the Zoo. They thought that what I did with the dogs I could do with wild animals. I could even have my own show. I refused. An unusual request came from the Police in Ottawa. Bush was coming and they considered my power very useful during the demonstrations. Again I declined."

"When did you lose your power?"

"One day a mutt appeared at my open garage door. I was sweeping the floor. He was a mixture of Black Lab and something else. He looked mad, as if he wanted to avenge the servile behavior of all the dogs I had made sit at my command. I shouted: "sit!" I said it twice. But nothing happened. Instead of sitting, he was getting closer and closer in a very menacing pose. The broom would have been my only defense. Fortunately for me, he retreated when the garage door started to come down. And that was it. I thought my magic power was gone for good."

"Did you try to use it again?"

"No, I had had enough. I didn't like the popularity. There was even an article in the local newspaper with my picture. I really like to know how they got my picture."

"Anyway you should be glad it's over. You were becoming a freak."

"Frank, sit down. I'll get you a beer. I'll be right back . . . I walked into the kitchen.

"Frank, what are you doing sitting on the floor?"

I thought Frank too had fallen under my spell . . . until I saw him smile. I helped him up half way and then I let him drop.

---

The hardest thing for an emigrant is accepting what he thinks are dangerous actions by the government of his country. For instance, I couldn't believe Berlusconi was still in power and some of his ministers were from the LEGA, a tiny party of buffoons from the North who felt superior to the rest of the country.

From abroad, we could only chastise them in our dreams until, fortunately, reality defeated them in the elections.

Mario and I decided to go to Cuba for a couple of weeks. Our wives were younger and still working, so they accepted the idea not to join us this time.

One gorgeous afternoon we were sitting at a table near the swimming pool, sipping cocktails and enjoying the breeze and the view of the waves, farther away, washing on the white sand of the beautiful Cuban beach. At a table next to ours sat a couple. From their conversation we could tell they were from Italy, for their Italian was much more fluent and polished than ours. They were both in their fifties. He was tall, fat and bald, she was slender and still attractive.

"Why don't we change subject?" She said to him. "Every time we talk about this, you get excited and it does not help your blood pressure. We are here to relax and enjoy the beach."

"Yes, it's true but if it had not been for that rascal of Garibaldi . . ."

When I heard him call Garibaldi a rascal, I jumped up ready to give him a piece of my mind. Mario grabbed my arm and made me sit down. He wanted to leave but I convinced him to stay by showing an apparent control of myself.

"What did Garibaldi do?"

"What did he do? He was responsible for the unity of Italy. The South was backward and different from us and has remained as such in spite of the flow of our resources towards them. Garibaldi didn't do us any favour by helping unite Italy; he wanted to make us pay for surrendering Nice, his home town, to the French."

I was seething with anger. Mario tried to calm me down. I turned to him and, in a low voice, I said that the North was not always rich and its present prosperity is also due to the work of thousands of Southerners who went North after the war to work in their factories. They also bought cars and machines from the North. Of course, Mario nodded in agreement.

The fat man at the next table continued. He complained about the many high officials from the South occupying good jobs in the North. She argued that many more educated Southerners won nation-wide contests for those jobs. He added that the North should have its own contests for the Northerners.

I stood up and Mario grabbed my arm again. I assured him that I just wanted to get away from there. As we were leaving, I saw the fat guy caressing her legs under the table. That irritated me even more. I thought that she deserved a better man. We walked and chatted about the subject. We both agreed that the guy was a nut but that perhaps a better federalism with a little more autonomy for the regions would be appropriate. The South would have to rely more on its own resources and initiative to catch up with the North. After the long walk on the beach, we stopped at a bar for a nightcap and went to bed.

I had a nightmare; I dreamed I had kicked the fat guy in the shin very hard. Mario heard my shouts of anger and came to calm me down.

Next day, after a long walk, we returned to our table. At the next table we saw the woman alone. We greeted her in Italian. She was surprised to hear us speak in her language and invited us to join her. We did. We ordered drinks and talked about many things, the beautiful beach, Guardalavaca the closest village, the proud Cubans, etc. Then I asked her where the husband was. She answered that the night before he had too much to drink, had fallen and hurt his leg, but fortunately it was nothing serious, only a swollen shin.

Far away the imbecile was limping slowly towards us. We took leave of her and headed to the closest bar.

Was it a coincidence? I'd rather call it divine justice. But can a dream really do that? I should try it on Berlusconi.

---

My professional interest in Latin America(I taught Spanish American Literature at the university) took me to different countries in the area. In the case of Colombia, I was usually accompanied by my wife who was born there. In one of our trips, I flew from Bogota' to the Colombian llanos on a small military plane landing in Araracuara on the banks of the Caqueta' River, about 250 miles from the border with Brazil.

I knew the danger. There were still bands of guerrilleros roaming in that area but Hernando, an officer and a friend of my wife's family, assured me that we would be safe, for more soldiers and helicopters had been sent there recently.

Hernando's wife is a friend of my wife. I accepted with some apprehension his invitation to go with him. My sense of adventure and my desire to see that wild region of Colombia overcame my uneasiness.

From the field airport we were driven to a Finca outside of the town where Hernando and other officers had their headquarters, which was guarded by soldiers. At dusk, after a few hours of rest, Hernando invited me to go with him to town. We drove in a jeep escorted by four soldiers in another jeep. We stopped at a bar "El Perico." The bartender greeted Hernando effusively and placed a bottle of aguardiente on the counter in front of him. I asked for a cold beer. It was hot even in the bar. We stayed there a couple of hours. Hernando ate chicharrones and drank aguardiente while asking many questions about people in town.

It had got dark and Hernando asked me to accompany him to a house. He said he knew two women who provided the Finca with arepas, sancocho, yuca, bocachico, empanadas. He said he visited them every time he came to Araracuara. He enjoyed the company of those two middle-aged women. Their very old mother was quite a character. He thought she was a little crazy. She liked to tell strange stories of the llanos and the Indians of the Amazonian forest. When she was younger she would get into a canoe and disappear in the forest. She would take with her a small wooden box. Nobody knew where she went, not even her daughters. She would come back afoot carrying the small box followed by two Indians carrying the canoe.

We sat in the patio. There was a full moon and it had cooled off a little. The two women brought empanadas and lemonade. Hernando offered the women aguardiente. He had with him two bottles he had brought from the bar. He sat between the two sisters joking and laughing loudly. He looked drunk. Then I saw him get up, go to the door, open the curtains and call:

"Doña Elvira! Doña Elvira!" and went back to his chair. A few moments later, an old woman appeared. She was tall and slender. Her long white dress enhanced her Indian features. Slowly she walked to an empty chair and sat. Hernando got up, went to her and deposited a bottle of aguardiente in front of her. He asked her smiling: "Doña Elvira, que' nos va a contar esta noche?" She didn't say what she was going to talk about. She sat dignified, her Indian skin shining in the moonlight. We waited a couple of minutes. Insects of all kinds whirled around. I lit a cigar hoping to keep some of them away. "Dolores, la copita!" she finally said. The daughter at the right of Hernando went into the house. She came out and handed her a glass. Doña Elvira filled it with aguardiente and drank it. Then she looked up to the moon and mumbled some words in a strange language. She looked around, waited a minute and said: "Mentiras!" I stirred in my chair and looked at her daughters. "Lies? Whose lies?" Two of the four soldiers entered the patio and sat on the floor. I noticed that Hernando had fallen asleep. "Mienten cuando cuentan que las Amazonas mataban a los niños varones." The Amazons did not kill the male children. They handed them over to the men who taught them to cook, clean and do many others chores and lived with the men in dwellings away from the sleeping quarters of the women. Female children, instead, were taught by their mothers to fight and hunt. She stopped talking to have another drink. She resumed her story: "Si', pues, eran muy valientes . . . " They were brave and fought well. Once they captured three "blancos." They castrated them and gave the genitals to the men to eat. Instinctively my hand went to the groin. She went on. They were never defeated, although it is true that Queen Macaba was captured and taken aboard one of the boats. They tied her hands but she managed to jump off into the swift current of the Japura' River never to be seen again. The captain didn't care. He must have been more interested in what he had wrestled from her: a golden girdle. She explained that queens in the forest did not wear crowns; they wore girdles.

She took another break to drink. A couple of minutes went by. I lit my cigar which had died out. The soldiers behind me were drinking; one of the sisters had passed them Hernando's bottle. They invited me to have a drink which I accepted.

Queen Macaba's girdle, she said, never made it to Spain. The "blancos" lost it in a fight with the Magochi Indians when their boat was attacked and destroyed. She had another drink and then she called: "Manuelita, traeme la cajita." The other daughter went in and came out with a small wooden box. She deposited it to her feet. Doña Elvira looked up to the moon and again she mumbled something. She opened the box and extracted a golden girdle. It shone in the moonlight. Then she got up, grabbed the bottle with one hand and with the other she slipped the girdle over the shoulder baldric wise(I guessed it was too large for her waist) and slowly walked to the door and disappeared inside.

The soldiers and I sat there in silence for a minute. On the jeep, on our way to the Finca with Hernando still asleep, I thought about Doña Elvira and her story. I couldn't help myself wonder whether the girdle was genuine . . . Of course, it couldn't have been . . .

In the afternoon of next day, I was given a ride to town. I went to "El Perico" where I had a beer while talking to the bartender who recognized me from the previous day. I asked about the old lady. He smiled. "Did she tell you the story of the golden girdle?" I was surprised to hear that he knew about that story. He then took out a bunch of golden girdles and laid them on the counter. I couldn't believe my eyes. There they were all shining like the one the old lady had showed us the night before. He told me that she would get them from an Indian tribe and sell them in town. She would leave some with him on commission.

Next morning we left for La Pedrera, on the border with Brazil. On the plane the night with Doña Elvira was still vivid in my mind. I asked Hernando why he didn't tell me that Doña Elvira was just acting. He replied that he didn't want to spoil the fun.

---

Dreams, dreams, dreams . . . where would the artist be without them?

It is a late Saturday afternoon and I am sitting on my favorite bench watching a few students pass by. I left the Memorial a couple of hours ago.

In our department Memorials have evolved somehow independently from those in other departments. Months must pass after the death of a colleague to give time to the members of the department to gather enough biographical facts. Of course, all the negative details are left out; then the chairperson is expected to find a general theme that would unify the eulogy and give a clear picture of the life of the deceased.

The first words uttered by the first speaker are always a celebration of life. In fact they go to an unusual extent to celebrate. There is a bar and a buffet and, of course, there is always a good crowd. By the time the speeches start, most people (some uninvited) have helped themselves to a few glasses of wine and something to eat. Customarily, the deceased's family members are first to speak. The widow or widower would only listen. I guess he or she would know too much and feel uncomfortable to talk only about the consort's good deeds.

I was sure that this afternoon the Memorial would follow the usual patterns. I hate Memorials but today I felt compelled to attend.

Nobody noticed me when I walked in, not even a couple of old colleagues. I felt invisible. Of course, most of the familiar faces have been slowly disappearing, replaced by younger ones.

The three sons and the daughter took turns in speaking about their father's life. I felt embarrassed when they started to reveal his private life. They talked about the man's fascination with stones. They mentioned how he would go down the ravine behind the house and bring back some strange stones. His house was full of them. From his trips to the old country he would always bring a few stones from his hometown. They all had holes in them and he would hang some in the patio. They haven't figured out what to do with them; perhaps some could be placed around his grave.

Their father enjoyed creating strange things that he would call sculptures. He liked to improvise them with minimum effort. Their backyard is a collection of weird figures made of scrap metal and wood. In vain he tried to make them see what he saw in them.

They talked about their father's love for unusual dogs: Bulldog, Dachshunds, Borzoi. The last one, Plato, a Boxer who was still with them, had a big problem. He salivated a lot and had large drooping jowls. When he shook his head it was like being under a sprinkler. Their father tried everything: helmets, muzzles, large coffee filters. Nothing really worked. He had to prevent the worst every time by rushing to hold his head before he sneezed or to wipe his lips right after he ate or drank. Plato's problem really drove their mother up the wall, especially since the time when a blob landed on her forehead.

Their father loved to own land. He bought some lots in far-away places even before he purchased his house. They guessed that it was due to the scarcity of land in the old country and the abundance of it here. They are still searching for the title to a piece of land somewhere in Prince Edward Island.

Soccer was his passion and when his country's national team played, nobody was allowed near him in the family room. He would light a cigar and every time his team scored he would drink from the bottle of cognac that he kept on his side. Once his team scored five goals and he got horribly drunk.

They continued to celebrate his life by revealing his amusing habits making everybody laugh. It bothered me particularly to see the widow laughing so hard that she had to wipe tears from her eyes. It was an undignified spectacle.

I had had enough of that celebration, so I left, making my way through the crowd. Again, nobody noticed me. I wandered through the streets of the campus looking at familiar buildings where I had taught for so many years.

Now I sit on my favorite bench under the old oak, evoking my life as a teacher. Things have surely changed since the introduction of the Student Evaluations. I learned to smile more at the students and I became more accommodating. No more ogling at beautiful female students, and I kept the office door always open to obviate false complaints of sexual harassment. A new era had begun.

Retirement was not such a big change. In our profession we always have free time. Of course, for a while I came to miss playing god in front of the class. But on the other hand, I enjoyed having the time to think, to evaluate, to read that book I never read, to write what I like. Now, I enjoy it even more. I am suspended in my own time, away from the world that controlled me, invisible to others.

A young student who has just sat on my lap has abruptly interrupted my reminiscences. I have asked her kindly to move over a little. She has not budged, so I have gotten up and moved on.

On my way out of the campus, I am thinking of the Memorial. Again I feel embarrassed for what they said and, in particular, for the widow's uncontrollable laugh still ringing in my ears. I take it very personally . . .

I am awake now . . . I think I should have a long talk with my wife.

---

I have finally taught Frank to drink either wine or brandy. This day it was brandy. We were sipping it out on the patio while playing cards.

"Play, Frank."

"Bob is not driving any longer . . . and he doesn't recognize me when I pass by. He sits there in front of his house staring at the old oak . . . He must be eighty or older. I think he is about to croak."

"The one to kick the bucket first, if you ask me, is Luigi. He must be of Bob's age. I don't see him working in the backyard any longer. His son waters the plants . . . He used to come around with a basket of tomatoes and we helped ourselves. Remember? Then he would sit with us and play a game of Scopa."

"Yes, but he is Italian and Italians have good genes, someone told me. Luigi is fat, though, and doesn't walk much now.

We sipped our brandy and kept on playing.

"Brigitte, that's the one to drop dead soon. She is all skin and bones and she doesn't leave the house any longer."

"Yes, I agree; she is a goner. I passed by her house a week ago. She was sitting on the bench by the door. I said "hi." She answered "piss off." Can you imagine?"

"She was beautiful."

We stopped playing. Old images came back.

"Yes, I remember. At Danny's house about twenty years ago she was sitting across from me in the backyard. I got a hard on looking at her half-parted thighs."

"Yes, even in her sixties she was attractive. But I think she is a goner now."

"Go ahead, play. It's your turn Frank."

"Let's drop this stupid card game . . . How old are you? I am seventy . . . We're also getting old . . . How's your prostate?"

"Shit, man, why do you have to bring it up. Mine is a little enlarged; how's yours?"

"Don't get upset; the reason I am asking about our age and our problems is that I am afraid some younger folks may be betting on us . . . who dies first."

"All we can do is keeping them guessing . . . for a long time ,I hope."

"I think life is a card game."

"I think it's a prank, Frank." We went in and sat in front of the TV. Bush was saying that Iraq had weapons of mass destruction.

# Drama

# HERE, ALL TOGETHER, KEEPING COMPANY

## A play in one act

The action takes place in a mausoleum but the real place is not revealed until the very end.

SETTING

A room with tables and chairs. A narrow window through which a ray of light will filter in the room, later. The burial vaults are at the back wall hidden from view.

CHARACTERS

Caterina
Filomena (widow)
Maria (Giuseppe's wife)
Concetta (Franco's wife)
He and She (young lovers)
Mario (youngster)
Boy
Two Girls
Vito (old man)
Giuseppe (Maria's husband)
Athlete
Giancarlo
Rosetta
Gianni
Mike
Franco
Pasquale

Corrado (gay)
A Black Man
An Asian

With the exception of the Boys, the Girls, Corrado and the Athlete, the characters are elders. They all dress in today normal fashion. The play requires some improvisation both in the typical Italian gestures and language which could also allow Italian words. Some characters are playing cards while others look on.

MARIA (dealing cards): Where are the other women?

ROSETTA: They're tired of playing cards. They're chatting some place.

CONCETTA: Gossiping, you mean.

FILOMENA (covering her mouth partly, whispering): Pinuccia, Giancarlo's wife, is always criticizing people.

CATERINA: She puts on airs. She feels superior because she is from the North. Quella si da le arie di gran signora!

MARIA: OK, play. Let her be. She can do whatever she wants; it's a free country.

CATERINA: He has had so much trouble with her. Do you remember when she wanted to go back to Italy?

MARIA: will you shut up? Concentrate on the game.

COCETTA: Scopa! (She laughs loudly).

FILOMENA: E brava. We get distracted and she makes "scopa."

CATERINA: But are we playing "scopa a vincere o a perdere?"

CONCETTA: Senza scherzi; we're playing "a vincere," to win, to win.

MARIA: Veramente, we didn't say . . . (to Concetta who has a serious face). But it's "a vincere," silly. Don't worry.

CATERINA: Ma che` ci giochiamo? Our husbands ? (loud laugh).

ROSETTA: Who wants them? They aren't good any more. (They all laugh).

CATERINA: If you search elsewhere, there isn't much to choose. Corrado . . . is out of the question. The Athlete has a nice body but he only thinks about training.

The young lovers, He and She, cross the room in a close embrace.

ROSETTA: Eh, beati loro! They are so much in love!

MARIA: But I feel cold. When will they put the heating on? It's November already.

VITO approaches the women. He looks at Rosetta's cards. Meanwhile men continue playing but their voices are very low. This allows the women's voices to be heard better.

ROSETTA (looking up to Vito who stands over her): Vito, please don't look at my cards because you bring bad luck.(She hides her cards from him). And don't start saying "Life is short, life is short." (Everybody laughs).

VITO: But why? Isn't life short?

MARIA: But we all know life is short but if you know how to live it, it doesn't seem so short.

VITO: Beh, I don't want to start an argument but for me even if you know how to live it, is always too short.

CONCETTA: OK. Now let us play. Go to them; they can tell you if life is too short or not. (Vito moves to where the men are).

MARIA: Scopa!

ROSETTA: Culo! Culo! Concetta e Maria always make "scopa." They are lucky!

CONCETTA: It's not luck. You have to know how to play.

ROSETTA: La fortuna e` dei ciucci!

MARIA: You talk and talk and don't pay attention to the game.

CATERINA (leaving the cards on the table and getting up to stretch): Basta, sono stufa. I am tired of playing cards. (Turning to Rosetta) Say, Rosetta, how do you make that dish of mussels, what do you call it? La pepata di cozze, if I am not mistaken.

ROSETTA: It's easy. First you clean the mussels under running water. Then boil some fresh tomatoes in salty water. You then cut them in small pieces and saute` them with oil, garlic and onions. E poi, you throw in the mussels. When they are all open add hot peppers. Cook everything for three minutes ed ecco fatto. E` una ricetta barese.

CATERINA: I like mussels but I have never done them that way. They must be really good.

MARIA: You always talk about fish. I don't like it. It makes me noxious.

COCETTA: Maria, have you ever made trippa? I learned to prepare it from my mother. She always used a very hot sauce.

MARIA: Your mother really knew how to cook. She also made a very good salciccia.

CONCETTA: Yes, she really knew how to make it. I have tried but it's too much trouble.


The Athlete goes by jogging. He is wearing a sleeveless shirt. Vito is now by the group of men playing cards. The women continue talking but their voices are very low. Sitting alone at some distance from them is Corrado. He has a sad face. The men are joking, laughing, shouting. Only a few are playing but everybody around them is commenting on the game. Mario, and the other boy and the two girls are also talking about the game.

GIUSEPPE: (addressing the youngsters): You mind your own business. Go and play somewhere else.

MARIO: And where do we go? We're bored.

PASQUALE: In my time, when we were with girls we were never bored. (Laughs).

GIUSEPPE (takes out a deck of cards from his pocket and gives it to Mario): Here, you can go play. Tell the ladies to make room at their table. (Mario puts the cards in his pocket but they have no intention of playing cards. Chatting and laughing they go out of the room).

MIKE (start to whistle the old fascist song): Giovinezza, giovinezza, primavera di bellezza, per il Duce Mussolini, ea, ea, alala` . . .

GIUSEPPE (with the cards in his hand): Mike, do me the favour: don't whistle that tune if you don't want me to get mad. Mussolini "fu uno stronzo" who ruined Italy.

MIKE: Italy was already ruined and would have been even more so in their hands. (He refers to Giancarlo who is now whistling the communist song "Bandiera rossa, alla riscossa, bandiera rossa trionfera`." He remains calm).

The women have left their table and have come where the men are.

MARIA: Beh, please don't start fighting; and you, Peppino (to her husband Giuseppe), don't get upset; you know is bad for your heart.

GIUSEPPE: But how can I stay calm when there are people who still believe in that villain of Mussolini. (Turning to Giancarlo). And you, Giancarlo, stop whistling "Bandiera rossa." You wouldn't have done better for Italy and you have no respect for the church,

GIANNI: But Giuseppe, explain me one thing: why you don't like people who reject Mussolini's ideas?

GIUSEPPE: No, this is not the point. I don't despise these people. Let's make it clear. I don't like Mussolini's ideas nor the Communists' ideas. I am a liberal and a Catholic.

PASQUALE: You are Catholic but you never went to church.

GIUSEPPE: How do you know? Were you spying on me? If I went or not is my business. I believe in God.(Turning to Giancarlo). They don't.

PASQUALE: You believe in God but have you ever asked him what we are doing here?

GIUSEPPE: Do you think I have his phone number? He must know why we're here and He will let us know when He will want to tell us.

FRANCO: If this is the place I feared, I don't find it that bad. Perhaps I deserve a worse place.

CONCETTA: I believe so.

FRANCO: You shut up! You weren't a saint either.

VITO: La vita e` breve.

FRANCO: Vito, you can't complain. You reached eighty . . . By the way, when is your birthday? I believe it is this month.

VITO: Yes, the 17th of November.

FRANCO: We will celebrate it here, all together.

PASQUALE (he has left the room to return with a guitar): Come closer and let's sing. (They are all surprised and ask Pasquale where he found the guitar). I heard him play during the day when there were no people around. He leaves the guitar in his closet in his room. (He plays and they all sing. This could last a few minutes, then everybody goes back to his place. Pasquale leaves the room to return the guitar to its place).

CORRADO (walks up to Mike and lifts his left hand to see the time on his watch. Mike withdraws his arm): I only wanted to see the time.

MIKE: Corrado, please don't touch me; I am afraid of getting infected. (They all laugh).

CORRADO: Terrone Cafone. (He speaks in a feminine tone).

MIKE (stands up furious): Son of the Padania. If you don't step away, I break this chair on your head.(He has lifted his chair in a menacing pose).

ROSETTA: Beh ,take it easy. ( The Athlete goes by jogging). Maybe a couple of runs with him would calm you down.

GIUSEPPE: Corrado, sit down but do not offend people.

CORRADO: He is always picking on the Northerners. If he insults us, I have to reply accordingly.

MIKE: Those who seek to divide Italy should be jailed

CORRADO (turning to Giuseppe): See the way he talks? You can't reason with him . . . (Turning to Mike) Here is my answer: The Padani are tired to support the rest of Italy.

CATERINA: Scusami, Corrado, but who helped make Padania prosperous? Weren't the Southerners also helpful? Who worked in your factories after the war?

GIUSEPPE: Silenzio! I thought I heard his steps. It's already daytime. (After a few moments of silence). No, I was wrong . . . Mike and Corrado, you as everybody here, see Italy from different points of view. But the fact that we speak so often of our country of origin means that we still love it. Each his own way but we love it. If we didn't love it we would not all be here keeping company. We share the same language, the same traditions . . . And now let's think about other things.

GIANCARLO: Do you know what would be good before retiring? A good glass of wine, even if just to smell the aroma.

MIKE: I never liked your wine. It was never as clear as mine.

GIUSEPPE: I prefer the white, a little "frizzante." I always made good white wine.

FRANCO: I prefer the red, "robusto, da pasto."

GIANNI: Forget the wine. What would be really good is an espresso like the one Maurino made. Remember?

PASQUALE: The real coffee was the one we drank in Bar Picicci . . . (Pause. Remembering). I would sit at the usual table with the "buon'anima" of Ciccillo with our cups in front of us, to see the game on TV . . . By the way, how's Cosenza doing? Here we need a good TV to see some games . . .


The names of the clubs could be changed.


FRANCO: Il Cosenza fa proprio schifo!

PASQUALE: E il Messina che fa? It's a joke, one step forward and two backward.

GIANNI: Pasquale, listen to me! Everything in the Italian League is a big joke. It is all about business now. Personally I don't like the increasing number of foreign players in the Italian clubs, specially in Inter, Juventus and Milan.

MARIA: Don't you ever get tired of talking about soccer?

GIUSEPPE: And you, over there, what do you talk about? It's always food . . . who makes better pasta, better sauce e come si fa questo e come si fa quest'altro. I tell you Maria, since you always brag about your ragu, I can tell you that Filomena's ragu is better than yours.

MARIA: And how do you know?

GIUSEPPE: Because I tasted it.

MARIA: Is that so? And what else did you taste? I like to find out. (She goes to speak to Filomena). Filomena, tell me something. How many times has Giuseppe come to taste your ragu and what else did he taste?

FILOMENA (with a worried look): Nothing else. Only once and he didn't even come in the house. He was sitting on your porch, so I invited him to taste my ragu. I gave him a small dish and he ate on my front porch. That's all. (Maria believes her and she sits next to her).

MARIA: Forgive me, Filomena. Sono una stupida.

CATERINA (to the men who are still playing): Don't you think it's time to quit? Why don't you think that it's November and they will soon be here to visit us . . . Silenzio! Now I hear clearly his steps! Turn off the light.

Corrado goes to the switch on the wall and turns off the light. In the semidarkness the characters freeze. They speak without moving. Long pause.

MIKE: If I had a chance, I would ask Nico, my son, if he has opened the two demijohns of the wine I made and how it tastes. I hope he has put it in gallons and is keeping them in the cantina, al fresco. I loved to have my friends over the house to test it over some slices of prosciutto and cheese.

PASQUALE: I would like to know how many bunches of grapes the vine at the side of our house brought and if they were as full and big as always. I wonder who prunes it and fertilizes it now. I did it every fall. When the grape was almost ripe, I would wrap the bunches in old stockings so the birds wouldn't eat it. L'uva mia era l'invidia di tutti.

CORRADO (with the effeminate tone of voice): I would like to ask Carmelo if he still loves me and whom he's with now . . . I loved the mountains in summer and winter. We would leave Pordenone and head for Bressanone or Merano. We would hike or ski. We loved it there. The landscape is unbelievable: mountains and lush valleys . . .

MARIA: Has our neighborhood changed? Agostino ,the butcher at the corner, the pizzeria on the other side of our road next to the Travel Agency "Sole Mio."

FRANCO: My car, 8 cylinders, old but very strong and no rust . . . I bought it new and it was a beauty . . . in the summer I would spend hours washing and waxing it. My wife loved to ride beside me and see people looking at our big car with envy . . . I wonder who drives it now.

GIUSEPPE: That grey heavy coat for cold nights like this; what did they do with it? I wore it in the fall and winter. I loved it. It was full of hidden pockets . . . They probably gave it away . . . my grey heavy coat.

CONCETTA: My little dog, Gigi, who woke me up every morning by pulling on the blanket . . .

ATHLETE: I liked to train running through the fields, up the hill; I would stop to drink water from the Torielli's well. Then running again. I was serious in my training.

MARIO: I never liked school but the last year I didn't mind it. Miss Luciani was nice and very beautiful . . .

GIANCARLO: I liked to go to the bar to meet friends and to talk about soccer, to hear the latest news, I nuovi acquisti, the referees . . . I remember one referee in particular. I think his name was Gallina . . . Yes, Gallina . . . and he looked like a chicken, una gallina spelacchiata . . . but he was good. He never made mistakes . . . oh, yes once he did, but he stopped the game, ran to the linesman to get his opinion and ran back to the field and changed his decision. Oh, yes, he was good, Mr.Gallina . . . But what I remember best was the day

Italy won the World Cup. I was so proud. I ran to my house, grabbed the Italian flag and ran out into St. Clair Street shouting: Viva Italia! Petto fuori, I sang "Sono un Italiano fiero." I went to the bar of Peppino and had a few grappa. I think I got drunk. At home my wife, Rosina, start to complain. I told her to shut up and I said: When did Italy win anything? She Shut up . . . Oh, yes, it was a great day!

ROSETTA: That big tree in front of our house . . . I asked them to spare it. It was there before the house was built . . . It always gave me a sensation of strength and peace . . . I hope it's still there, with the squirrels on the branches and the bird nests . . .

FILOMENA: That cottage on the lake . . . so welcoming in the summer. We would meet there so often . . . So many sacrifices to build it . . . It was a shack when we bought it. Whom would it now belong to?

CATERINA: That beach where I met him and where we made love . . . I would like to see it again and run barefooted on the sand, throw flat pebbles to see them skip the water . . . to lie in the sun . . .

GIANNI: Those two paintings that I finished before I retired; where would they be now? I would sit in front of them to admire them. I liked particularly the one showing the lake in the North with an island in the middle . . . Maybe I had talent for painting . . .

VITO: She wanted to be cremated and asked me to scatter her ashes on the beach of Alba Adriatica. I did that and I remember it was very windy . . . (Pause). Her feet were always cold and in bed she liked to rub them against mine . . . (Pause). My little hometown . . . I hoped to go back . . . to die there . . . I didn't make it . . . Life is so short.


The morning light which filters through the window finally exposes the burial vaults on the back wall. They had been hidden by the curtain. All the characters walk very slowly towards the back wall. Only the Lovers move downstage.

SHE: Today you will let me sleep with you, right?

HE: Of course, Love, we'll sleep together. (They walk in a tight embrace and move to the Stage right.)

The voices of a Black Man and of an Asian are heard. The two men are not visible.

BLACK MAN: I wish there were more Blacks here. We would have a ball every night. None of this "giocare alla scopa." We would dance till dawn.

ASIAN MAN: I don't know . . . I would prefer a session of Tai Chi every night.

BLACK MAN(laughing): No, man, no. It's boring.

ASIAN MAN: Not for me. It keeps you fit . . .

CONCETTA (whispering to Rosetta): Did you see who's behind us? We thought this place was only for Italians! We have to complain. They never told us they would allow other people in here.

ROSETTA: One finds out when it's too late.

ASIAN and BLACK MAN: It's never too late!

Vito turns around. The other characters remain with their back to the public.

VITO: I will remember by myself today also . . . my memories and I . . . Life is short, there is no doubt . . . but it leaves memories so long, so long that they never end.

This play was first staged at St. Michael's College of the University of Toronto in 1999. It was presented again in Mississauga, Ontario, at the Burnhamthorpe Library Theatre, in 2006. The songs in this second presentation were Mi votu e mi rivotu (a Sicilian melody); Reginella Campagnola (an Abruzzi melody) and a Tarantella.

Translation of some words:

Scopa a vincere o a perdere, p.38 Trans: the winning scopa or the losing scopa. To win in the losing scopa, one should try to pick less cards and not to score points. "Scopa" is an Italian game played with Italian cards.

Ma che ci giochiamo? p.39 Trans: What do we play for?

Culo, culo . . . p.40 Trans: ass, ass. To have the luck of the devil. To be lucky.

La fortuna e` dei ciucci, p.40 Luck helps those who don't know how to play.

Ed ecco fatto, p.40 and that's all.

E` una ricetta barese, p.40 It's a Barese (from Bari) recipe.

Giovinezza, giovinezza, p.41 Youth, youth. A Fascist song.

Bandiera rossa, p.43 Red flag. A Communist song.

Mussolini fu uno stronzo, p.44 Mussolino was a turd.

Terrone cafone, p.44 Peasantboor. Derogatory terms used by Northern Italians to offend Southern Italians.

Frizzante, p.44 Sparkling

Robusto, da pasto, p.44 Full-body, mellow.

E come si fa questo e come si fa quest'altro, p.44 And how you do this and how you do that.

Sono una stupida, p.45 I am stupid.

L'uva mia era l'invidia di tutti, p.45 My grapes were the envy of everybody.

Gallina, p.46 Chicken. His real name was Collina, a well known Italian referee.

Petto fuori . . . sono un Italiano fiero, p.47 Chest out . . . I am a proud Italian.


Most of these words are not essential to the action. Their function is to stress the ethnic aspect of the play.

# The Case of Clara Bellucci

This play contains music, dance and some fanciful costumes. There are three musical pieces : one is associated with the supernatural; the other two, one in Scene 2 and one at the end, lead to dancing. In the last scene drums are heard briefly.

SETTING

The play takes place in a North American city, today.

Stage setting

A permanent architectural set, subdivided in two parts: CLARA's living room and CAPO's office. The former would occupy a wider space. The small partition between the two spaces could be easily removed. CLARA's living room has two doors, one leading to her bedroom. The action goes back and forth from CAPO's office to CLARA's living room. When one part is illuminated the other remains in semi-darkness. A few times complete darkness is required. In Act III two more settings are created.

CHARACTERS

CLARA, about 35, voluptuous, spunky and undergoes a spiritual change. She has a slight accent.

PERI, the young devil, nice-looking, naïve.

GOLI, the angel, gender neutral between male and female, blonde, experienced.

CAPO, an older devil, dressed in black. He operates his devilish enterprise with an alert business-like manner.

CARMELA, same age as Clara, also pretty.

MEN and WOMEN in line at the soup kitchen.

OLD LADY behind the counter at the soup kitchen.

FOUR DEVILS, also dressed in black.

HIGH MAGISTRATE OF THE INDEPENDENT COUNCIL (HMIC), about 50, dressed in a combination of two colours, half in black, half in the golden colour of the angels.

CLERK, dressed as the HMIC.

FIVE DEVILS, dressed in black. Two are females.

FIVE ANGELS, dressed in tight-fitting golden suits. They are all blonde.

DEVIL, in CAPO's office.

VOICES, in ACT II

ACT I

Scene 1

The supernatural music invades the stage as the curtains open in a dimly lit room with a small desk and computer with a few chairs facing the desk. It may remain in the background or it may disappear completely. This is CAPO's office. Behind the desk sits CAPO, in charge of the devils' operation in town. He has a goatee and is dressed, like the other devils in the play, in a black turtleneck sweater and jacket. He addresses PERI who sits in front of him and he is taking notes.

CAPO: Let me tell you about Clara Bellucci. Clara is a special case. Most people accept the angel on their side and totally ignore us and we cannot tolerate it. But Clara is different . She treats both equally because she realizes they are an integral part of her being. She is a realist. You hear her often say that life is made of both good and bad and why not have the respective representatives at one's side to consult and discuss the choices one makes so often in life . . . She believes that the two opposite aspects make life more interesting. Can you imagine life made up only of saints? It would be very boring. Peri, that kind of thinking is helpful to us because that is precisely the space where we need to move in a person's life. Yes, that situation makes it more fair and gives it just the right balance. (CAPO gets up and begins to pace). As you know, you're here to replace Pala. She got tired of Clara; she could not convince her to sign anything. Of course, there were no complaints about Clara's loose behavior but Pala was anxious to have her signature so she could move on to another job . . . Perhaps there was some jealousy on her part. Pala envied Clara's freedom. I explained to her that we don't get involved emotionally. It's dangerous. It can hinder our mission . . Anyway, she's been assigned to another woman . . . an older woman . . . I wasn't pleased with her performance and for her sake I hope she will improve in the future. (CAPO moves close to PERI, confiding). Normally I would not give an assignment like this to a first-timer . . . but, you are recommended and although Clara has been moody and very difficult, I think the timing is right to have her commit to our side; behind her façade of gaiety and self-confidence, Clara is a little confused. She is now toying with Buddhism and the teaching of the Dalay Lama . . . I believe she would like to change her life but she doesn't know how . . . You have to deal with Goli, the angel assigned to her. Be careful with him. He is an experienced angel . . . You may wonder why the rush if everything is going our way. Well, you see, these so-called sinners can sin all they want but they can repent even at the last minute of their lives and then we get nothing. So, the sooner we get them the better.

PERI: Can you please tell me more about Clara?

CAPO: She is a widow. She's around 35 and still beautiful. Her husband brought her over from Europe when she was seventeen and three years later he died in an accident leaving her penniless but she learned fast how to survive in the new country. Now she is in a profitable trade. Her beauty allows her to choose her clients, those with money, of course.

PERI: Mr. Capo, what is her profession?

CAPO: The oldest and very profitable profession. She sees clients, special clients and they have to be to her liking . . . So, it's neither money nor men that may induce her to sign a pact. She has enough of both. It's up to you to find out what other wishes she needs to fulfill. One never knows what people wish for. You see, some of our clients' wishes are outlandish but we always try to satisfy them . . . We had a case of an old man who wished for a continuous supply of Montecristo cigars and Cognac, but he forgot to ask for a longer life. He died of lung cancer the following year. (Capo laughs.) Another man wished to be rich to attract beautiful women. We granted his wishes. (He's laughing loudly.) Women were attracted to him but only to his wealth and status. He forgot to ask for the power to physically satisfy them. (Laughter.) He tried to have the contract revised saying that we had deceived him, but as you know, our policy is not to change contracts and we are skimpy on details and provisos of any sort. We do well among the scoundrels, the destitute, the very poor, the bag ladies, the peddlers, etc. They're always easy to sign on. People are mystified when they recognize them as bank presidents, politicians and doctors after having seen them on the streets. However there are many cases when we are helpless, when a person's faith makes our job very difficult. But we must always try, for it is our mission. And then there is Clara . . . a tough case. You will have your hands full.

PERI: Is there anything else I should know?

CAPO: There are borderline cases in which we are not sure if we are trespassing. It happens when the wishes come from the heart and the heart has always been our number one enemy . . . Sorry, I strayed a little . . . what else do you need to know about Clara? Only this . . . as I said before, be careful with Goli, the angel assigned to Clara (PERI gets up, ready to leave. CAPO puts his hand on PERI's shoulder)

Good luck, Peri. Get Clara to sign and I will make sure your next assignment is a good one.

Lights dim to black. As they come up in CLARA's living room, we hear her melody. She's in her negligee, soothing in a pensive mood. The music increases in tempo and she smiles. She lurks up and the stage is filled with fog-like clouds. Sensing the mood of the music, she begins to dance about the room. The fog-like clouds slowly disappear. She recomposes herself, lowers her eyes realizing that she had been dreaming about some strange but appealing goal in her life. She is now within the reality of her living room and needs to deal with earthly matters. There's a knock.

CLARA: (someone knocks again.) Who is it?

PERI: (Offstage) I am your new devil, replacing Pala.

CLARA: I am not in the mood to receive anyone tonight.

PERI: I am your devil . . . replacing Pala.

CLARA: No. I am going to bed; good night.

PERI: I'll be brief, only a moment, please.

CLARA: Only a moment! (CLARA hesitates, then opens the door) As you can see . . . come in. (PERI enters) So Pala gave up, eh? What's your name?

PERI: Peri.

CLARA: Aren't you kind of young for this job?

PERI: This is my first assignment. (They both sit.)

CLARA: You have a slight foreign accent. That's strange for a devil.

PERI: I was in Italy for one year at a training centre. They have the best place for devils. I enjoyed it very much. Se vuole, possiamo parlare in Italiano.

CLARA: No, I prefer to speak in English. My Italian is very rusty, e` un po' arrugginito. Sorry about Pala but I am glad to be watched over by such a handsome young devil. (She smiles.)

PERI: Thanks for the compliment but I don't expect to be around here long. I hope to convince you to sign a pact as soon as possible.

CLARA: Well, don't be in such a hurry. Pala must have found out I am not so easily persuaded. After all, my soul is at stake. Besides, I am not living a life that you devils wouldn't approve of . . . It's him you should be worried about. (She points to GOLI who has just entered from the backdoor. He wears a shining, tight, golden outfit.)Goli, meet Peri. He is replacing Pala. She gave up. (There are no handshakes.) Excuse me but I have to go to bed, to my own bed. Peri, please stay; Goli will keep you company. (CLARA and PERI rise. CLARA shakes PERI's hand.) It's a pleasure meeting you. See you soon. (She exits smiling. The supernatural music rises and then recedes.)

PERI (ready to leave): Well, I might as well go.

GOLI: No, no; stick around. I want to take a good look at you . . . You're young. Why did they send you here?

PERI: I don't know. It's my first job and a difficult one. It's going to be a challenge.

GOLI: Clara is a tough case, even for me. Don't be too concerned. She's going your way. She does not listen to me anymore.

PERI: Yes, I know, but things can change

GOLI: So, you'd rather be completely sure by having her sign a pact. It's too bad we don't have that option. We can only try to persuade, encourage, enlighten . . . you, however, can just waltz right on in, offer her the world, have her sign on the dotted line, and voila! She is yours for eternity.

PERI: Actually, I think you guys have it easier. A person can be terrible all his or her life, I mean a true monster, and then, at the last second all he/she has to do is repent and bingo, he or she is off the hook. Think of it: some poor devil gets assigned a case, puts in years of hard work ensuring that his case is an awful person, then at the last moment, all his hard work is wiped out as the person repents and converts over to your side.

GOLI: You have a point. (Pause) What do you plan to offer?

PERI: I am not at liberty to discuss it.

GOLI: She'll never sign as long as I'm around.

PERI: Well, we'll see about that. (PERI gets up and leaves.)

A Minute of Darkness. Light on CLARA's living room. CAPO's office remains in semi-darkness

GOLI and CLARA. She's wearing an elegant dress and is sitting on the sofa. Goli is standing behind the sofa. She's reading.

GOLI: You're going to another of your rendezvous. (CLARA ignores him.) . . . What are you reading, if I may ask?

CLARA: It's the Koran. Everybody is reading it now . . . you know, from what I read so far, Islam does not seem so different from other religions. It preaches belief in one God and even in the angels.

GOLI: True. We also help them.

CLARA: I was also struck by the Islamic morality, specially regarding the sharing of wealth with the poor . . . Tell me, Goli, if all religions believe in helping the poor, how come there are so many poor people in the world?

GOLI: Don't go.

CLARA: I must go. (She gets up and looks at her watch.) It's late.(Holding a small compact mirror, she checks her make-up, grinning.) You are welcome to come with me.

GOLI: I'd rather not.

CLARA: Yes, I know. You would be ashamed . . . Today is a big day for me. He is a rich man in town on business. We've already met. He's married but he likes me very much and he treats me very nicely . . . As you know, I don't come cheap. He knows it too . . . I know you don't like my living like this, but you forget that I had no choice . . . My husband left me without anything here in this foreign land. All I had were my good looks . . . But I have money now. I don't have to do this for much longer. Who knows, you may even become proud of me after I quit.

GOLI: You tried to quit before but your resolutions are always weak. All I can do is pray for you to amend your ways . . .

CLARA Oh, don't start giving me that godly talk. ..How do I smell? Do you like my perfume? Well, good-by; see you later. (She goes to him smiling and pinches his cheek with two fingers. She exits.)

Scene 2

GOLI is now alone. He walks around in a pensive mood. The supernatural music is heard. The door opens and PERI appears.

GOLI: Ah, it's you again . . . You don't go with her because you approve her conduct; I don't go because I would feel ashamed. So, here we are: the two antagonists facing each other while the subject of their antagonism is out having a good time.

PERI: My job is to see that she does not turn your way and to make sure she remains faithful to us forever. We have no complaints so far but everything can happen, especially now that she is well off and she does not have to sell herself . . .

GOLI: Yes, yes. I understand. We keep an eye on each other. But you have an advantage: the diabolic pact, the power to satisfy her material needs in return for her souls. Anyway, we both know where we stand and what's at stake . . . (pause.) The problem is that this job can be very boring at times . . . What do we do while we wait? We can kill each other. (Loud laughter) . . . Do you like music?

PERI: I don't know.

This scene is bizarre. The supernatural music fades away. GOLI claps his hands and the room fills with a new, strange, rhythmic music. He begins to dance slowly with movements that seem more contortions than dancing steps.

PERI: What are you doing?

GOLI: I am dancing. Don't you see? Haven't you seen dancing before?

PERI: I have never seen anybody dance, let alone an angel.

GOLI: You really are green. Why don't you try it? Come on; follow my movements.

PERI gets up and tries to imitate GOLI. GOLI shows him how to dance but it is obvious that he is not a good dancer himself. Both move around with strange movements, separately. This goes on for a few minutes until the music subsides, it remains in the background. They sit.

GOLI: Well, what do you think?

PERI: It was OK, I guess.

GOLI: What do we do now? Oh, I know: let's play a game of cards.

PERI: What's that?

GOLI: I'll show you. (He goes and gets a deck of cards. They sit around the coffee table.) This game is called "managi." It's very easy. Each tosses ten cards in the air and then we add up the numbers on each card that turns up and whoever has the higher number wins. Look! (He tosses ten cards about twenty inches in the air and then he counts the numbers.) Forty-two! Now you try. (PERI does the same.) Fifty-five! Peri, you won! You sure you have not played this game before?

PERI: Never.

GOLI: Let's try again. (PERI wins again.) You're very good. You beat me twice . . . let's bet something. That'll make it more interesting. Let's see . . . Whoever wins this time is allowed to be alone with Clara for 30 days. The other will not show up for that entire period of time. How about it?

PERI: Well, I don't know. I'm not sure Mr. Capo would approve.

GOLI: Oh, come on; forget Capo. You're doing well. Come on. You start.

PERI: Well, OK. (He tosses the cards; they count.)

GOLI: You won again! You're very lucky! I can't win one . . . but I have a hunch you played this game before and that you are putting me on.

PERI: I've never played cards before.

GOLI: OK. Let's raise the stakes. What would you like to bet on? (Pause) How about we bet on Clara's soul?

PERI: Are you crazy? I can't do that. Mr. Capo would have a fit. He would give me a lousy assignment.

GOLI: You surprise me. I always thought you devils were proud of your independence, your boldness, daring and imagination. Your original defiance gave you the reputation of free thinkers and daredevils. Forgive the pun. (Long pause as PERI thinks about this, then . . . )

PERI: Let's play!

(They play and PERI looses.)

GOLI (getting up): Sorry, old pal. You're out of Clara's life . . . she's mine. I'll be back in thirty days. (He exits smiling at Peri. The music rises dramatically. PERI, dumfounded, stares in the emptiness. A couple minutes go by. Then slowly he gets up and exits. The music fades out, lights dim to darkness.

ACT II

Scene I

Lights will stay out for some minutes while some voices are heard.

VOICE I (sincere): My darling Clara, it's always a pleasure. Here's the money I owe you. You may not know it but you've really helped me. You taught me how to be intimate again. Even my wife has noticed a change in me. I wish you good luck. I am sure you won't stay in this business too long.

VOICE II (boisterous): Clara, have a drink with me. It'll cheer you up. Salute! (Pause) What's the matter? Where is the passionate Clara I know and love? . . . I have an idea; why don't we go away, take a nice little cruise in south sea . . . just the two of us. (Pause) I have never seen you like this. What's the matter? Are you getting involved with someone seriously? Will you not see me again?

VOICE III (British accent): What's the matter? You are not your usual dominating self. I paid good money to be your slave. I want you to punish me. I've been a very bad boy . . . Why don't you punish me?

VOICE IV (a woman): Clara, I love you . . . I think about you day and night. I just want to be with you. Why won't you talk to me?

VOICE V (angry): Mother treats me better and I don't pay her anything. I just sit there and the old bag talks and talks and touches and touches . . . (angrily) I wish Old Bendy would take her . . . You have changed, Clara. Does it mean we won't see each other again?

VOICE VI ( confused): What's wrong with you today? We always had a good time . . . You know exactly what I need. But you seem . . . in a hurry. This is not going to work. You're not the same. You've changed, Clara.

Light on CAPO's office. The supernatural music is heard briefly. PERI is sitting in front of the desk. CAPO is pacing the floor with his hands crossed behind the back. A few moments of silence.

CAPO: I am very disappointed. Weren't you told to be careful with experienced angels? You should have known better. I warned you to be cautious around Goli . . . Here . . . (He rushes to the computer on the desk and presses a few keys.) Come and see. He used the same trick three other times. (PERI remains seated.) But he is not getting away with this! Goli did not act in good faith and neither will we. In one of your card games you won the right to be alone with Clara for thirty days. So, you have thirty days to convince her to sign. Offer anything . . . I am afraid I have to be blunt with you: if she does not sign in thirty days you may be assigned to a job you may not like. You see, I have to respond to my superiors too . . . Now, before you go, I want you to meet some productive comrades. (He pushes a button and four devils enter the room. They are all dressed like CAPO and PERI; all have vacant stares and strange smiles.) Sit. (They all sit still smiling.) Do you know, Peri, how many souls they gained in one year? Fifty! . . . They specialize in drug-addicts. They meet them in dingy coffeehouses and dark back-alleys. They promise them hard drugs and return with signed contracts. The men and women use the drugs in high doses and die; it's as simple as that. No waiting around as you do with Clara. (He turns to the four and signals them to leave. They leave still smiling. It's obvious that they are hooked on drugs also. A pause. CAPO looks at PERI, then, with a conciliatory tone of voice, he adds.) To be honest, I think they like their job too much. They are hooked on drugs like their clients. They will not be able to carry out any other assignment. But as long as they are productive . . . Anyway, I don't think you would like to join them. Would you?

PERI: No, I wouldn't.

CAPO: I know you wouldn't . . . In a way their job is easier. People like Clara are not easily persuaded. It has become a test of will for all of us. As you know, we have the reputation of being very persistent . . . We are interested in finding out how long she can hold out . . . Your success or failure will be studied by our superiors and changes could be made . . . Anyway, what is important now is that you take advantage of Goli's absence. For thirty days Clara's is yours. Go now.

A minute of darkness. CLARA's living room. CLARA is drinking a cup of coffee and eating a cookie. PERI is sitting across from her. Clara's music is heard before they start to speak.

CLARA: Would you like an espresso?

PERI: No, thanks.

CLARA: You're not saying much. What's the matter? (Pause.) Tell me, Peri, how bad is hell?

PERI: Hell? What's hell? I've never heard of it.

CLARA: I mean the place where you come from, where sinners are sent. It's supposed to be in the bowels of earth, where souls are condemned to eternal fire and boiling water.

PERI: There is no such a place, as far as I know. We do not dwell in one place. We are everywhere. After death, the so-called sinners are sent to us instead of going to Him and enjoying His presence. We train them to be like us. Some become devils like me and mingle with humans. If you look around you may see them in many places. They are usually dressed in black .(Looking at the audience)Some even go to the theatre.

CLARA: So, if I am not good, the punishment is not being allowed to see and be with Him. But how long does this punishment last?

PERI: Until He decides to let all of us join Him.

CLARA: Even you?

PERI: Even us. We were created by Him. Meanwhile we concentrate on the mission imposed on us: to take as many souls as we can and to keep them from seeing Him. We rely on our cunning and perseverance and on some supernatural powers. But, as you can imagine, we are not always successful.

CLARA: I am a little confused. You oppose Him on earth but at the end you'll join Him. I guess He made us ignorant so we could never fully understand all these mysteries . . . Thank you, Peri, anyway. (She gets up.) I don't know what happened to Goli. It's really strange. I haven't seen him for over two weeks . . . Do you think he got tired just like Pala? But I can't say I miss him too much. He reminds me of my youth, my innocence and I am not young or innocent any more . . . It still hurts to remember that time and how it all ended when I left home to come here . . . (A few seconds of pause.) But let's talk about you. Do you know why I treat you as a friend? Because you're part of me. Many people don't want to acknowledge the presence of the devil in their lives, but I do . . . (Smiling.) Do you know you're a very handsome devil? How are your feelings toward women? Do you find me attractive?

PERI: I don't know . . . our feelings are not human, although sometimes we get carried away. But we are constantly warned against any emotional attachment. It can hinder our mission . . . I have to go. (He gets up.)

CLARA: No, no, please stay. I won't ask personal questions again. Let's talk about your mission. It's about the surrender of my soul in exchange for a great favor. Right? I talked with Pala about this matter but I never took anything she said seriously. Above all, I was not sure about what I really wanted as part of the bargain. We were going nowhere and that's' probably why she left.

PERI: I have been empowered to be very generous in satisfying your wishes.

CLARA: Really? (a little sarcastic.) Let's see now. What do I wish for? A husband? No, I already had one and I am too independent to have another. Money? I don't think so. I am not doing too badly. I own this house and I have money in the bank . . . So, what is that I may wish for that I don't have? (A moment of silence. She seems to have discovered a deep feeling in her. She is now very serious ) You know, Peri, maybe God permits evil in order to draw forth some greater good . . . It would be so good to change my life now, to be that greater good. (Absorbed.) Yes, to help others.

PERI: Not another Mother Teresa, please.

CLARA: (ignoring PERI's words): These last two weeks I reflected a lot, also because I quit my job and I had more time to think . . . Peri, believe it or not, there has always been an hidden idealistic part in me that believed in goodness . . . It would be great if I could help the needy without anything in return . . . (looking at PERI, surprised of her own words.) I know it's unbelievable, still it feels good bringing it all out, telling someone about it.

PERI: That someone doesn't like what he's hearing.

CLARA: Yes, I know. You didn't expect to hear this. Good deeds you'd rather not hear about. You see, Peri, as strange as it may sound, in my profession love has not been a complete stranger . . . it has been bruised and debased at times but it has remained alive inside of me. Just last week I asked myself why I still visit a client of mine who has been in hospital for over a year . . . I didn't have to do that; I don't owe him anything. And anonymously I have been giving money to people in need whom I meet on the street . . . But one can also help in other ways.

PERI (getting up as if to leave): Clara, look. There is no reason for me to stay here any longer. I am going. I'll come back another time.

CLARA: No, no, Peri. Please, don't leave. Have a little more patience. (She invites him to sit again. ) About three months ago, the wife of a man whom I had been seeing occasionally found out who I was. She came through that door like a wildcat, shouting obscenities, pushing and scratching. I let her blow off steam till she collapsed on the sofa crying. She was a beautiful woman but beauty alone does not keep a husband faithful. When she calmed down, I started to talk to her and we talked for a long time. After a few questions, she opened up. Her husband was no saint, by any means; but she had her faults too. She admitted that her relations with her mother, sisters and her interest in her father's business often took precedence over her marriage. She realized she needed to find a balance between her emotional attachments. We had tea and she left. Now she calls me once in a while to invite me to lunch or to go shopping. Her marriage is working out fine . . . I often ask myself what made me act like that instead of throwing her out on her bum when she walked through that door. You see, Peri, I have been a call girl with a heart. I have a subconscious desire to be good.(Grinning) Yes, I'm a call girl with a heart.

PERI: I don't know why I am here listening to you. Yes, you are a call girl with a heart but Mr. Capo said that the heart is our number one enemy.

CLARA (becoming more and more passionate as she speaks). Love is very much alive in me. All it needs is a chance to be used in its purest form towards others. Yes, Peri, humans can change if given the opportunity . . . Although the cost will be high, I am ready to take that chance. I have been thinking a great deal about the power of signing a pact with you . . . I can have anything in exchange? What if I asked for the ability to do good in exchange for my soul?

PERI: I think I understand what you're getting at, but I am sorry, your wish is out of my jurisdiction. You forget who I am. We prefer the way you were . . . We rather satisfy material desires. What you're asking is in the other side's domain.

CLARA: The other side doesn't believe in granting wishes. They rely on our natural goodness and free will. But life is short and hard and our goodness takes a beating. Long established habits and the need for security and comfort do the rest . . . To carry out this change in my life I need support. Alone I may not be able to succeed and that's where you come in, Peri. If you don't want to do anything, I will ask Goli. In exceptional cases the angels may ask for some divine intervention.

PERI: Please, Clara, leave Goli out of this. Give me some time. Let me talk to my superior. I'll come back with a definite answer. See you later. (PERI exits. The lights fade except a spotlight on CLARA who stares in the void. Then darkness.

Scene 2

CAPO's office. Supernatural music. CAPO addresses PERI from behind his desk.

CAPO: A call girl with a heart? This is not good. The heart is our number one enemy. We must tread carefully here. I guess I didn't stress enough the possibility of change in her, but I wasn't sure when and if her hidden idealism would overcome her materialism . . . But now we have to deal with it.

PERI: She even suggested she would ask Goli.

CAPO: Blackmail... Well, Goli is not around and we have a chance to get the contract signed. Yes, Peri, let's go ahead. Tell her we agree. The signed contract will invalidate Goli's win. As for the ethicality of the deal, we'll let the Independent Council decide, if it comes to that. Goli must feel confident; he thinks we have given up. We haven't and we will not.

PERI: I will go and let Clara know that we agree to her proposal. ( He exits).


A moment of complete darkness Clara's living room again. A knock on the door. Clara opens the door and invites her friend Carmela in.


CLARA: Come in, Carmela. I am so glad to see you.(They kiss and go and sit on the sofa) It's been a while since I had a woman to talk to.

CARMELA: What ever happened to that friend of yours Poola, Peely... that you mentioned?

CLARA: Pala. She left. She got tired of trying to convert me. (She serves Carmela her tea) I was just having some tea or would you prefer coffee.

CARMELA: Thank you. Tea is fine. Was Pala a religious fanatic?

CLARA: In a way. Let's just say that she was a spiritual advisor.

CARMELA: Are you still seeing those two friends you said you see from time to time? Are they also spiritual advisors?... Clara, this spiritual stuff... I don't get it. To be frank, I think they come to your house for sex and they use the spiritual story to have it at your house... You never had clients at home before.

CLARA: Goli and Peri are not clients and they are not interested in sex. Let's leave it at that. OK, Carmela?

CARMELA: Clara, I have to confess you look different. You're more serious, less expansive. I remember you so happy, so full of life. I can't forget the day we went out, you and that friend of yours and my husband and I. We really had a ball . . . and that Halloween night when you dressed as a vampire. You scared the hell out of my daughter Marisa . . . You're not the same, I tell you . . .

CLARA: I have retired from my line of work.

CARMELA: Hallelujah! (jumping up from the couch, arms in the air) I am so proud of you! I knew the day would come (She kisses Clara's cheek passionately) Brava! It's those Asian religions you have been studying, isn't it?

CLARA: Well, I have been reading a lot lately. Some books are very enlightening. After comparing the teachings of different religions I have come to the conclusions that most religions are very similar in their message; it is the way they are practiced that is different; you must cover your head, or let your beard grow, eat fish on a certain days, or don't eat pork, etc. To me these practices seem inconsequential; what is truly important is what is in your heart.

CARMELA: You really sound like a changed person.

CLARA : I am not the same. I search for meaning . . . our true purpose. Everything used to be so material to me; I had to hold it in my hands to appreciate it. But not anymore. I used to think that you could cheat in business, cheat on your partner, be a dishonest cop, a corrupt politician, a call girl . . . and still be virtuous, be redeemed by doing some good deeds, giving to charities, going to church, giving money away. I'm not sure I believe that anymore. I think it's convenient to believe that. Sometimes I am overwhelmed with a desire to change in a way that is . . . profound. I want to renounce everything that is no longer important and commit myself to only doing good, to only being good. But then I think of the sacrifice that is required (pause) and I don't know if I have the strength.

CARMELA : Maybe Golpi and Peggi can help?

CLARA: Goli and Peri . . . yes, I am counting on one of them to help me. (They sit quietly for a moment, looking at each other)

CARMELA: Perhaps, you can tell them to come and see me also.

Darkness. A minute of silence. Clara's living room. Her music is heard again. A knock at the door. Clara answers.

CLARA: Peri, I didn't expect you so soon.

PERI (walking into the room): I talked to my superior. We agreed to fulfill your wish in return for your signature. (He hands her the contract.)

CLARA (taking the paper and depositing it on the coffee table. She looks unsure of herself): Since you left, I've been agonizing over the whole thing . . . It's a big step and I am going to ask you to have some more patience and to give me more time.

PERI (a little surprised): I know it's a big step, even for us . . . but if that's what you want, I leave the contract with you and I will see you later, but please don't take too long. (He exits)

Complete darkness.

Intermission

ACT III

Scene 1

CLARA's living room. CLARA's melody reappears. A knock at the door. CLARA opens the door revealing PERI

CLARA: Come in, Peri. No, this time you won't be disappointed.

PERI: I hope so. Capo has become very impatient. We never expected your decision to take this long. Capo has threatened to pull me out of this case and who knows where I'll end up. I have been doing small jobs here and there but your final acceptance of the deal will help me a lot.

CLARA: Yes, I know. It has taken a long time. But this time you didn't come in vain. Capo will be happy. I have decided to go through with it in spite of the high price . . . It's ironic I would turn to you, Peri, but you're offering the only guarantee I won't revert to what I used to be. Alone I wouldn't be able to become the virtuous person I want to be. In return for my soul, you are allowing me to live the rest of my days promoting others. I wonder what Goli would think? (She picks up the paper that Peri had left on the coffee table. Then she sits down to read it once again before signing it).

PERI: Has Goli been around?

CLARA: No, he hasn't. Which is strange. He never stays away this long. Do you think he knows about the contract?

PERI: I don't know; but he will know when the time comes.

PERI (he picks up the contract handed to him. He looks straight in Clara's eyes. The stare lasts a few seconds)

PERI: Goodbye, Clara. (He stares at her once again and then he leaves.)


CLARA 's tune fills the room and then slowly fades away. Darkness. The lights would stay out a few minutes to give time for changing the setting.


We are in a soup kitchen in a shelter for the homeless. CLARA and an old lady are behind the counter serving a line of men and women. CLARA is wearing a plain black dress. One man, clearly under the influence, of alcohol, reaches out trying to touch CLARA's breast.

She backs away. PERI, appearing from nowhere, steps up and with a powerful swing knocks the drunk senseless. Two men, without knowing what happened to him, pick him up and carry him to a table. The drunk is out and remains seated with his head down on the table.Nobody seems to notice PERI, except CLARA. She serves him soup smiling. After serving a couple more people she joins him at the table.

CLARA: Thanks for your intervention but it was not necessary.I know how to deal with them. But thanks anyway . . . So, what brings you here? I am not dead yet.

PERI: I wanted to see you, see how you were doing.How are things going? Have you adjusted well to this new life? Do you have any regrets?

CLARA: Peri, I don't feel anything.I carry out my daily charitable work routinely. I know I am helping people but I am doing everything automatically, like a machine. The good I am doing does not reverberate in me.

PERI: Does it mean you're not happy?

CLARA: I am not happy or unhappy.I don't feel anything.I guess my feelings did not count at the signing of the contract.

PERI: That's possible. Our contracts are intentionally vague. We leave out as many details as possible.You asked to lead a new life, totally immersed in goodness and we granted it. Nothing else. (PERI is not eating. A homeless man takes his soup and bread.)

CLARA: I appreciate your frankness . . . Is there any way to renegotiate the contract?

PERI: I am afraid not.

CLARA: I have to get back.Nice seeing you again, Peri.Stop by any time. I am always glad seeing you.(She gets up and goes behind the counter.)

PERI: Likewise, Clara. See you. (CAPO appears. He sits opposite to PERI). Mr. Capo, why are you here?

CAPO: Once in a while I like to go around to see how my staff is doing . . . You clubbed him pretty good. (He laughs). He is still out. I should ask the same thing of you: why are you here? Never mind.I know.

PERI: I was curious to see how she was doing . . . Mr. Capo, she complains that she has no feelings, that her good deeds don't affect her one way or the other, that her feelings were not taken into consideration.

CAPO: Ah, yes, the regrets . . . Humans don't look at their future situation in details. They regret it later. There is no denial that the lack of details in the contract is to our own advantage. If they thought seriously about all the situations they would find themselves in the future, many would not sign.

PERI: Is it possible to renegotiate the pact?

CAPO: Peri, do I note in you some attachment to Clara? You know very well we don't get attached.The answer, of course, is no. (They get up and leave.)


GOLI appears.He approaches the counter.He cannot be seen except by Clara.


CLARA: Goli, what a surprise! I haven't seen you for quite some time. (They go and sit at the table.) I thought you had been reassigned to another case.

GOLI: No . . . well, I was busy with minor duties . . . but let's talk about you. I am really glad that you changed your life. My prayers must have helped.

CLARA: Goli, what helped was Peri's willingness to guarantee that

I would have the strength to go ahead with my wish to change and never to revert back to my old life.

GOLI (jumping up): He didn't have you sign anything, did he?

CLARA: Yes, I signed a contract.

GOLI: But it was out of his jurisdiction, way out. Besides, you were already mine.

CLARA: What do you mean I was yours? I didn't belong to anyone.

GOLI: I won your soul at a card game.

CLARA (furious): Did I hear right? You won me at a card game? You mean you and Peri sat down and decided to bet on my soul? How arrogant, how absurd . . .

GOLI: Peri's contract with you was also facilitated by a card game. He won the right to visit you without any interference from me for 30 days and it was during those 30 days that he had you sign.

CLARA: I can't believe I'm hearing this. I am conditioned by the contract to be good, but this is too much. (Standing up) Get out and never come back! ( He leaves. CLARA is crying).

Lights dim in CLARA's living room

Supernatural music. CAPO's office. CAPO is behind the desk shuffling papers. A Devil is doing the same. He is sitting near CAPO's desk and his papers are stacked on another chair next to him.

CAPO: Can you believe it? They claim his signature is false. He used somebody else's name . . . I can't find his contract.

DEVIL: It's not here. I looked at these papers twice. Do you think that it may have been filed by mistake under the forged name?

CAPO: I don't think so.(He keeps on shuffling. PERI enters).

PERI: She is dead. (CAPO does not pay attention to him).

CAPO: Keep on looking. It must be here some place.

PERI: She died in an accident. (He is standing in front of CAPO).

CAPO (finally looking at PERI): What are you talking about? Who died?

PERI: Clara Bellucci.

CAPO: So? She signed the contract, didn't she?

PERI: Yes, but the contract may be contested. We may be called to defend our case.

CAPO: I am sure you'll put up a good defense. You'll be fine.

PERI: If there is a trial, will she be there?

CAPO: I don't know. She might.

PERI: Is there anybody who could take my place?

CAPO: Don't be silly, Peri. That's a preposterous request. That's your case, Peri. You deal with it. I am again warning you against . . .

PERI: Yes, I know: against compassion, love, involvement . . . But if you deal with humans every day some of their humanity is bound to rub off on you.

CAPO: Rub it off, Peri; rub it off. (Pause.) If you win the case, she will be one of us and you would be happy. Now, let me work. I have a lot to do. We have a missing contract. (PERI exits. CAPO goes back to the file).

Complete darkness. A couple of minutes to clear the stage. "Supernatural" music.

Scene 2

All the furniture is gone. Only one chair for HMIC. He has his back to the public. CLERK is on his side, also with his back to the public. CLERK and HMIC are dressed alike. Their costumes and their hair are partly black and partly golden. There are two separate groups in the room and they are facing HMIC and CLERK. One group is composed of five angels. They wear the same golden shining costume as GOLI; in the other group there are five devils, two of them female, and they wear the same black costume as PERI. PERI and GOLI are in front of their respective groups. The music stops abruptly when CLERK starts to speak and a soft beat of drums is heard.

CLERK: The Council is in session. The Highest Magistrate of the Independent Council is presiding. (The drums stop and the supernatural music is heard but it stays in the background.)

HMIC: Today we are here to assess the validity of two claims, both concerning the soul of Clara Bellucci. Goli (he points to him) maintains he won it fair and square over a card game. Peri (he points to him) on the other hand, alleges that Clara's soul belongs to him, since she signed a contract. In return, she was granted her desired state of goodness for the rest of her life. She died in an accident a month ago on her way to deliver food to a family. Peri, what do you wish to add?

PERI: Your Highness, Goli knew he would win the card game. He did it three other times to my comrades. The records in your possession attest to that. I had never played that game before. On the other hand, Clara Bellucci signed the contract of her own free will.

HMIC: Goli, what do you have to say?

GOLI: Your Highness, Peri took advantage of my absence for thirty days. Clara Bellucci committed herself to sign during my absence. Peri won the right to be alone with her also over a card game. Clara wouldn't have signed if I hadn't been forced to be away for thirty days. So, if my win is not valid, his shouldn't be either.

HMIC: We heard what Goli and Peri had to say and I have reviewed all submitted evidence. I will now give my opinion. Your approval (pointing to the two groups) will sanction it. Anybody who disagrees after hearing my opinion should step forward. (A few moments of silence.) I believe we have to dismiss Goli's claim, for it's undignified to use a soul as a stake in a card game . . . In regard to the pact signed by Clara, it would appear to follow the rules; she wasn't coerced by Peri to sign. However, the question we have to ask ourselves is whether the contract was ethical . . . (pause.) It seems to me it was not, because the fulfillment of Clara's wish of becoming an unselfish and generous woman was not in Peri's domain; it was in the angels' jurisdiction, although as we know, seldom they apply that prerogative. Therefore, since Peri was acting improperly, the pact is not valid. Do you agree with my opinion? (Murmurs of approval from both sides are heard.) We are now left with the dilemma of what to do with Clara Bellucci's soul.

The background music stops. From the back, CLARA, wearing a long white dress and with her face covered with a veil, walks slowly between the two groups toward HMIC. She stops in front of him, on her sides are standing now GOLI and PERI.

CLARA: Your Highness, since the Council is deciding my fate, I think I have the right to be present. (Movement of heads in approval from both groups.) In my last year my behavior was conditioned by the contract which now has been found to be invalid. Therefore I am asking your Highness to restore me to life as I was before the contract. I don't regret having done good deeds but it wasn't I who was doing them. It wasn't Clara. It was the contract that dictated how I was to behave. I want to be myself again, free to make my own decisions, free to choose between right and wrong, free from outside pressures. Now I know that if I decide to be completely virtuous again I will never ask anybody for help. And if I hear that someone is betting on my soul, I'll punch him or her till kingdom come.

(Murmurs of approval.)

HMIC (glad to have found a solution. After a short pause): We are in agreement. Clara Bellucci, by the powers vested in me, I now declare you "alive". (Murmurs of approval.) I am glad our dilemma is solved. (He is smiling.)

CLARA (she casts off her long white dress and her veil. She is now wearing a short tight skirt): Thank you, your Highness.

A strange music with a strong beat fills the room. CLARA starts to dance. She shakes her body following the beat. PERI and GOLI do the same around Clara. The five members of each group start to dance also, first among themselves, then intermixing with the members of the other group. CLERK is dancing with HMIC. Then, suddenly, the music stops but, with the exception of HMIC, they all keep on dancing.

HMIC (turning to the audience): Clara was quite a woman; don't you agree? I am sure you're anxious to know how she lived the rest of her life and where her soul went after she died. Unfortunately all I am permitted to tell you is that she was judged by a higher court. (He bows.)

The music rises again and everybody, including HMIC, is dancing until the curtain falls.

THE END

———